Scotland

Books by W. A. Poucher
available from Constable

The magic of Skye
The Scottish Peaks
The Peak and Pennines
The Lakeland Peaks
The Welsh Peaks

Other books now out of print

The backbone of England
Climbing with a camera
Escape to the hills
A camera in the Cairngorms
Scotland through the lens
Highland holiday
The North Western Highlands
Lakeland scrapbook
Lakeland through the lens
Lakeland holiday
Lakeland journey
Over lakeland fells
Wanderings in Wales
Snowdonia through the lens
Snowdon holiday
Peak panorama
The Surrey hills
The magic of the Dolomites
West country journey
Journey into Ireland

SCOTLAND

W.A.Poucher

Constable London

First published in Great Britain 1980
by Constable and Company Limited
10 Orange Street London WC2H 7EG
Copyright © 1980 by W. A. Poucher
Reprinted 1981
Reprinted 1982
ISBN 0 09 463860 8
Printed and bound in Japan by
Dai Nippon Company, Tokyo

The photographs

Preface

During the last forty years I have travelled the northern hemisphere in search of nature's beautiful and dramatic scenery, and have done my best in favourable weather to photograph it. I have used for this purpose both Kodachrome and monochrome with my two Leicas and a Leicaflex, together with a wide variety of lenses.

I have, of course, been greatly impressed by such spectacles as the Grand Canyon, Arizona: I was the first Englishman to descend it on foot, sleep beside the Colorado River, and ascend its steep walls to ground level again next day, in eleven hours. I have also enjoyed the splendour of the Canadian Rockies during a summer of glorious sunshine, and was especially charmed by the wonderful turquoise colour of its lakes. Nearer home, I have explored the graceful, soaring Alps and the colourful Dolomites; and in Britain and Eire I have spent months each year walking their delectable valleys and climbing their peaks. When asked which of all these places I consider the most beautiful, I have confessed my preference for the north-western Highlands and the Isle of Skye.

I have written and illustrated in monochrome some thirty books portraying the magnificent scenery to be found by exploring our hills and dales, but this is the first one in colour, and I hope it will not only please my Scottish friends but also the thousands of readers of my other pictorial Guides which cover Wales, the Lake District, Skye, the Peak District, and the Pennines. Readers who are interested in mountain walking and climbing will find a complete account in my *Scottish Peaks* of the safe ascent of the hills pictured herein.

To anyone who knows Scotland, the plan I have adopted for this book will be obvious. But for those who are not so fortunate and wish to see for themselves the best of Highland scenery from a car, this work will be an indispensable guide, as one scene follows another in the order of their appearance from south to north, and then south again. Moreover, it will be clear that my greatest interest as a mountain photographer is in the portayal of nature's masterpieces, rather than in the works of man; although in a few pictures, such as those of Shieldaig and Ullapool which have a special charm, I have included them for that specific reason.

W. A. Poucher
4, Heathfield
Reigate Heath
Surrey
1980

The Arran Hills from Brodick

These hills occupy the northern half of this beautiful island and the three ridges are dominated by Goat Fell. This peak can easily be ascended by anyone who is fit, and the walk to the north along its summit ridge opens up the finest views of the central ridge backed by the distant sea.

The Pinnacled Ridge of Goat Fell

(overleaf)

Walking along this lofty ridge on a clear sunny morning reveals a splendid prospect of the most picturesque peaks of Arran.

Ben Vorlich from Loch Lomond

Dominated by Ben Lomond, this loch lies almost on the doorstep of Glasgow and is a prize for lovers of beautiful scenery. It is the largest sheet of fresh water in Britain, and covers an area of nearly twenty-seven and a half square miles. While the island-studded lower reaches of the loch are largely given up to water-sports of all kinds, its upper reaches are narrow and altogether more charming to the eye. The road along its western banks yields the finest scenery, of which this photograph is typical.

The Cobbler

(overleaf)

This is the name given by the climbing fraternity to Ben Arthur which rises to the north-west of Loch Long. Its weird serrated profile at once stamps it as the most striking peak in the southern Highlands, and it is well seen from the railway in the vicinity of Arrochar. Its summit ridge can be reached by a good path from Succoth, but the central peak involves some rock climbing and should not be attempted by the lone walker.

Ben More from Strath Fillan

This beautifully shaped mountain is a conspicuous landmark throughout the length of Glen Dochart and Strath Fillan, and, together with its equally graceful neighbour Stobinian, affords one of the easiest ascents in Perthshire, provided always that the atmosphere is clear and the peak is not snowbound. It is the highest peak in Britain south of Strathtay, and in consequence discloses a stupendous panorama on a clear day.

Ben Lui
from Cononish

(overleaf)

This is the most shapely peak in the southern Highlands, and this viewpoint can be reached by a level Forestry Walk of about a mile, from Tyndrum Upper Station. The ascent of Ben Lui is not recommended for the ordinary pedestrian.

Stob Ghabhar from Loch Tulla

The southern peak of the Blackmount frowns
upon the head of this lovely loch, which is seen
at its best from the by-road to Victoria Bridge.
Stop Ghabhar is the first hill to be climbed when
making the magnificent traverse of this fine
mountain group.

The Blackmount from Rannoch Moor

(overleaf)

Any traveller driving from Tyndrum to Fort William cannot fail to be impressed by the vast desolation of Rannoch Moor, as the new Glencoe road passes through some of the grandest scenery in the Scottish Highlands for no less than thirty miles. Of these, about twelve miles consist of wild, undulating moorland, triangular in shape and stretching from Loch Tulla to Altnafeadh, with its apex on Loch Rannoch. Those who have tried to walk across it in any direction will have some conception of the Moor's immensity and of the pitfalls that are unexpectedly encountered; for it is intersected by many burns, cradles some large lochs and innumerable small lochans, and abounds in peat hags and areas of impenetrable bog. To attempt to cross it in clear weather is a hazardous adventure, but in rain and mist it could spell disaster. In fact, to be parachuted into the centre of Rannoch Moor in such conditions would present a problem of escape to test the stamina and skill of our toughest and most experienced commandos. Yet on a sunny day, Rannoch Moor is resplendent with wild beauty, engirdled by mountains and decked with glittering sheets of water, which, together with boulders strewn about and great masses of heather, make a picture that appeals to both artist and photographer.

This picture shows the most spectacular view of
the Moor from a roadside lochan.

Sron Na Creise from Kingshouse
(overleaf)

Here is a splendid view of the terminal peaks of the Blackmount as seen from Kingshouse. This hostelry, on the old Glencoe road, is an excellent centre for the exploration of the Glencoe district.

A charming lochan in Glen Etive

Perhaps the most picturesque feature of this long
and lovely glen is the small lochan portrayed
here. It lies some distance to the left of the road
and may be reached by a sketchy path which
terminates in a fine mass of rhododendrons, seen
at their best in May.

Buachaille Etive Mor emerging from the morning mist

(overleaf)

This shapely peak is known as the 'Shepherd of Etive' and is seen at its best from near Kingshouse. It is famous for its many difficult rock climbs and is a favourite with all mountaineers.

The Three Sisters of Glencoe from the Old Road

On a clear day these peaks are seen by everyone
passing through Glencoe, and are the crowning
glory of Argyll. All of them delight the climber,
but their ascent is not for the ordinary walker.

Aonach Dubh
from Clachaig

(overleaf)

Crowned by Stob Coire nan Lochan, this is the
third of the famous Sisters and is seen at its best
from Clachaig. The break in the centre of the
cliffs is known as the 'Dinner-time Buttress', and
it affords a quick ascent for the experienced
climber.

Aonach Eagach – the North Wall of Glencoe

This spectacular ridge is one of the narrowest
and most exciting in the central Highlands. But
its traverse is the special preserve of the
experienced climber, and, once on it, there is no
escape from the crest except at either end.

Loch Leven and the Pap of Glencoe

(overleaf)

Instead of crossing the new bridge at Ballachulish, it is worthwhile driving round this beautiful sea-loch. It opens up a succession of lovely views of the enclosing hills, including the Pap of Glencoe which is the western sentinel of Aonach Eagach.

The Mamore Peaks from Glen Nevis

The reward of a drive from Fort William to this glen is the superb scenery for which it is famous. On approaching Polldubh the first glimpse of Mamore Forest is disclosed, with Sgurr a'Mhaim and Stob Ban topping the skyline, as seen in this picture.

Polldubh Falls in Glen Nevis

(overleaf)

These fine falls cannot be seen from a car. The visitor must park beyond the last wooden bridge, and walk down the steep bank on its left, when the falls will be revealed *under* the bridge.

Ben Nevis from Banavie

The enormous bulk of our highest mountain
overlooks Fort William, but its most interesting
elevation can only be seen by driving to Banavie.
Here, by the late afternoon light, it is revealed in
all its glory, with the Glen of the Allt a'Mhuilin
hemmed in on the left by Carn Mor Dearg and
on the right by the towering cliffs of Coire na
Ciste.

Ben Nevis from Corpach

Corpach village lies at the southern end of the
old Caledonian Canal, and its buildings on the
pier make a charming foreground to the view of
the great Ben on the other side of Loch Linnhe.

Early morning in Corpach

(overleaf)

This is a good viewpoint for both artist and photographer who delight in portraying the atmospheric effects of early-morning *contra jour* lighting.

Loch Laggan

This loch is some twelve miles in length, and its
waters are used as a reservoir by the British
Aluminium Company at their works outside Fort
William.

Golden days in Glen Garry

(overleaf)

Before the level of this loch was raised, it was famous for the birches which decked its northern shore for miles. Unhappily thousands of them perished in the process, and one can only hope they will grow again in the coming years, to reproduce this lovely golden tapestry.

Loch Hourn

A superb drive of about twenty-five miles, from Invergarry to the narrow head of this spectacular arm of the sea, is one of the finest in Scotland and should on no account be missed. The road runs along the full length of Loch Garry and, after passing the remote Tomdoun Hotel, yields a glimpse on the left of Loch Poulary, before reaching the dam at the foot of Loch Quoich. Thereafter it crosses miles of undulating moorland, with the loch close beside the road, and, after leaving it, enters the foothills surrounding the still-undisclosed Loch Hourn. Then, quite unexpectedly, it turns spectacularly left, crosses the face of the cliffs (well protected

Faochag and the Saddle from Glen Shiel

(overleaf)

The drive down this famous glen is a delight, with the hills closing in until the two peaks shown here appear to block its exit. However, on crossing the Bridge of Shiel the road bears right to skirt the flanks of the Saddle, until the waters of Loch Duich appear ahead. This picture is the classic view of the wild scene.

by an iron rail) and descends steeply, with views ahead now of the loch, to its shore. This loch, usually regarded as the most magnificent in all Scotland, is dramatically enclosed by high hills which fall precipitously to its narrow and remote head.

The Five Sisters of Kintail from Mam Rattachan

This mighty range of hills dominates the head of Loch Duich and its conspicuous, well defined tops can be picked out among the cluster of its neighbours from many points to the west. Its finest elevation is revealed from the crest of Mam Rattachan, where the view includes the blue of Loch Duich below. The steep drive up to this superlative belvedere requires care, but the rewards are immense, for the Five Sisters are there revealed to perfection. Their lofty traverse is one of the joys of tough mountain walkers.

Plockton

(overleaf)

This charming village on the shore of Loch Carron is worthy of a visit, and can be reached most easily from the Kyle of Lochalsh.

The Satellites of Beinn Bhan

During the descent to Loch Kishorn by the hill-road from Loch Carron, this fine mountain scene comes into view. On the right of Sgurr a'Chaorachain stands the Cioch, a famous problem for the rock climber. The spectacular road to Applecross starts below them at Tornapress, and in a distance of only six miles it rises from sea-level to a height of 2,053 feet at the Bealach na Ba, its final zigzags climbing at a rate of 1 in 3. But the road is safe, and is a must for touring motorists.

The Mural
Precipices of
Coire na Feola

(overleaf)

One of the magnificent corries that flank the northern slopes of Beinn Bhan, it can be reached by an easy walk from the bridge at Tornapress.

Beinn Damh from Lochan an Loin

The single-track road to Shieldaig passes this
small lochan, which is one of the viewpoints that
best reveals the long summit ridge of Beinn
Damh. A remarkable feature is the strange
'Stirrup Mark' below the summit, whose
prominence is due to white quartzite scree.

Shieldaig

(overleaf)

This fishing village is a favourite with all who pass by, and walkers are glad of some accommodation here. From the lofty road to Kenmore there is a fine distant view of the village.

Beinn Alligin from the River Balgy

Rising in Loch Damh, this famous river flows
down to Loch Torridon through five salmon
pools.

Beinn Alligin from Upper Loch Torridon

(overleaf)

From the higher stretches of the Shieldaig road this picturesque mountain is revealed at its best. It has two remarkable topographical features – first, the long gash falling from the reigning peak, and second, the adjoining Horns of Alligin. Its complete traverse is not difficult and is much enjoyed by the hill walker.

A ruin in Glen Torridon

Even a ruined cottage can make an attractive
picture in favourable conditions, but sadly this
one has now been removed.

The Coulin and Beinn Damh Forests from the Diabaig Road

(overleaf)

One of the most beautiful drives is to the remote village of Diabaig – the single-track road runs for miles high above Loch Torridon, and from it can be seen many peaks of the Coulin and Beinn Damh Forests, of which Beinn Damh is the most prominent.

A telephoto shot of Beinn Damh

This picture demonstrates the use of a long-focus
lens, which is a valuable gadget for any
photographer.

The Village
of Diabaig
(overleaf)

Remarkably situated at the foot of high cliffs, this cluster of fishermen's cottages terminates the picturesque drive from Torridon.

Liathach from Loch Clair

Travellers who go to Scotland in search of scenery on the grand scale will not be disappointed because the Highlands are graced with so much of it. Glen Torridon is one of the finest glens of all, and should on no account be missed. Ten miles long and threaded by a single-track road with passing places, it extends from the village of Kinlochewe at one end to Upper Loch Torridon at the other. Here, on the shore of the Loch, stands a beautiful hotel which, as Beinn Damh House, was the original home of the Earls of Lovelace. As a frequent visitor I got to know the fourth Earl very well, and he told me that he owned about 96,000 acres of the glen and its adjoining hills, but had given up trying to make them a paying proposition. He had experimented with sheep, and then with cattle, but as the ground was all rock, covered scantily with grass and heather, this had failed, and he had been forced to the conclusion that the glen was of interest only to the stalker, the salmon- and trout-fisherman, and the mountaineer.

From this description it will be clear that Glen Torridon is a magnificent valley, its real grandeur being owed to the three great mountains that hem in its northern side. They are faced on the south by a collection of lesser, but nevertheless striking, peaks. Most of them are of red Torridonian sandstone, often capped with white quartzite; they are terraced horizontally and extremely steep. The most majestic and imposing of them all is Liathach, which extends for six miles beside the road and whose narrow summit ridge is no less than five miles long. Its traverse is for the experienced mountaineer only. Walkers who wish to penetrate the fastnesses of these sombre and silent hills will find a splendid stalker's path running behind Liathach.

The Terraced Wall of Liathach

The unique southern wall of this great mountain
is only clearly revealed to both eye and camera
late on a sunny afternoon, when the low angle of
infra-red rays throws into sharp relief its
extensive mural sandstone precipices.

A rainbow in Glen Torridon

(overleaf)

I was descending the sandstone ledges of Beinn na h'Eaglaise on a showery afternoon when this exquisite phenomenon appeared, and as suddenly disappeared. In these transient conditions any photographer has to be quick with his camera if he is to achieve success.

Beinn Eighe from Loch Coulin

Some half-way along Glen Torridon there are two lovely lochs. Loch Clair lies beside the road at the foot of Beinn Eighe (which is the largest of the Torridon peaks, and a complete range in itself) and to the south of it lies Loch Coulin, which may be reached by a level private road. Loch Coulin is the best place from which to appraise Beinn Eighe, as is shown in this picture. The great mountain is scenically outstanding for two reasons: first, tremendous areas of white quartzite scree are draped over its higher slopes and glitter like snow on a sunny day; and second, Coire Mhic Fhearchair lies on the north-western extremity of the range and is undoubtedly the most magnificent in all Scotland.

A clearly marked path rises gently from the car-park in the glen, passes through the narrow

Beinn Eighe
from Kinlochewe
(overleaf)

After leaving this village by the Torridon road there is a bridge at Cromasag where the view of this section of the mountain is unobstructed by trees. And while it looks magnificent under snow, it also appears very splendid at other times of the year because of the gleaming white quartzite which covers the whole of its lofty ridge.

gap between the two adjoining peaks, and steepens as it approaches the corrie. It is hard going for the elderly and takes about two hours, but the rewards are immense, for its three buttresses, of which the lower halves consist of red sandstone and the upper halves of white quartzite, rise into the sky on the far side of the corrie to frown upon the lonely lochan at their feet.

93

Slioch from Grudie Bridge

This well-known bridge is six miles from
Kinlochewe and is a good viewpoint for Slioch,
whose bold, square, castellated summit looks
most attractive under snow. But in summery
conditions it is clearly seen in splendid isolation,
dominating miles of the upper reaches of Loch
Maree.

Loch Maree

(overleaf)

Before the construction of the new road that keeps well above the upper reaches of this beautiful lake, a narrow road flanked with silver birches hugged its shore and opened up many lovely aspects of its rippling waters. The wider foot of the loch, with its tree-clad islets, has made it famous as a paradise for anglers.

Gruinard Bay

After leaving behind the attractive gardens at
Inverewe, the road enters a long section of wild
country, often flanked by the sea. Its jewel is the
lovely bay which suddenly appears far below, at
a bend where cars may be parked. Beyond it, on
the distant horizon to the right, is the first
glimpse of An Teallach, another of Scotland's
great mountains.

The heavenly blue of the Bay

(overleaf)

A calm day, with a cloudless sky mirrored in the immense expanse of Gruinard Bay, is a sight that will never be forgotten by any passing traveller.

The coast beyond the Bay

The little promontories and gleaming sands of
the small bays beyond Gruinard Bay make them
an alluring place to linger, either for a walk on
the sands or perhaps even a bathe on a sunny
day.

An Teallach from the Road of Destitution

(overleaf)

This great mountain range, with its lofty pinnacled ridge, is seen at its best from the road a few miles to the east of Dundonnell. Its traverse is one of the mountaineer's treasured experiences, but should not be attempted by ordinary walkers.

Ullapool

This fishing village, with its white cottages fronting Loch Broom, is one of the most attractive places in the far north of Scotland in which to stay. Walkers find it conveniently situated for exploring the Coigach peaks, a collection of enticing hills which can be climbed safely by anyone who is fit. In good weather, a sail to the Summer Isles is a further delight.

Ben More Coigach from Ardmair Bay

(overleaf)

One of the most beautiful bays in this part of the Highlands, where a few isolated cottages stand on the curving shore that leads the eye to the long ridge of Ben More Coigach. This can easily be traversed by any fit walker.

Ben More Coigach from a Drumrunie Lochan

This sequestered little sheet of water lies beside
the road and can easily be missed by a motorist
driving fast. When its gleaming surface is still, it
mirrors all the surrounding peaks: one of them is
seen in this picture.

Stac·Polly

(overleaf)

This little peak can now be easily ascended by the zigzag path on its northern slopes, enabling visitors of any age to reach its summit ridge. The bristling sandstone pinnacles make it an irresistible subject for the photographer, who in favourable weather can capture them backed by many blue lochans far below. There is a car-park at the starting point of the ascent. This picture was taken on an autumn afternoon, whereas the frontispiece was photographed from the summit ridge on a March morning.

Cul Beag from Loch Lurgain

The placing of the boat on the sandy shore of
the little cove makes the picture.

The coast road to Lochinver

(overleaf)

Motorists driving north from Ullapool have the option of two routes to Lochinver. The quickest is by Inchnadamh and Loch Assynt, while the slower but more adventurous road turns left at Drumrunie. Some years ago the latter was a risky drive, owing to the lack of passing places in the narrow and twisting section beside the sea. But this has been remedied, and its curves now make for a most attractive journey.

The road descends to the sea

This photograph shows one of the surprising
views afforded by the road to Lochinver.

Inverkirkaig Falls

(overleaf left)

After leaving the sea, the road rises to a good viewpoint and then falls again to the River Kirkaig, where a car may be parked. The walk beside the enchanting burn is delightful, and leads to the falls seen in this picture.

Suilven from Lochinver

(overleaf right)

This famous peak is unique and stands in splendid isolation amid the wilds of Sutherland, five miles to the east of Lochinver. Its lofty, narrow ridge is one and a half miles long, and is the special preserve of the mountaineer. But any pedestrian of any age can walk in its shadow along the path in Glen Canisp, passing many a shining lochan and with a fine view of Suilven's neighbour Canisp ahead.

Canisp and Suilven from the Drumbeg Scenic Drive

A picturesque drive starts at Lochinver and circles the coast to the north, passing the remote hamlet of Drumbeg, crossing the moors to Skiag Bridge, and returning along the shore of Loch Assynt. It unveils many lovely views of the sea, and a visit to the lighthouse at Stoer is a worthwhile diversion. This photograph was taken in retrospect from the first hill on the circuit.

The road beside the sea

(overleaf)

This is a typical view on the early stages of the Drumbeg Scenic Drive.

The hamlet of Drumbeg

This inn is famous and much patronized by
artists whose paintings may sometimes be seen
on its walls. Quinag is in the background.

Quinag and Ardvreck Castle from Loch Assynt

(overleaf)

Lochs and lochans of great charm and in beautiful settings are dotted about all over Scotland, and many of them are an irresistible magnet for salmon- and trout-fishermen. It would be invidious for me to declare any one of them the most beautiful, but I always take a special delight in visiting Loch Assynt. It is dominated by the great mountain of Quinag, and is also famous for the ruin of Ardvreck Castle which stands on its shore – Montrose was confined there in a dungeon before being taken to Edinburgh for execution. There is a good hotel at Inchnadamh near its head and another at Lochinver not far from the outflow of this lovely Sutherland loch. Scenery on the grand scale can be enjoyed by driving in any direction for a few miles: perhaps the drive to Kylesku is best of all.

An islet in Loch Assynt

This is one of the many beautiful islets that deck
this tranquil loch.

The River Inver

(overleaf)

Famous for its salmon, this river takes root at the outflow of Loch Assynt and reaches the sea at Lochinver. In my early days it was common to see no cars other than Rolls-Royces and Bentleys parked beside it at the favourite beats for salmon-fishermen. But not so today. On a sunny autumn afternoon, its waters flow through a golden tapestry of great beauty, and lead the eye to the Sail Ghorm ridge of Quinag.

Sail Gharbh from the Kylesku Road

The magnificent drive from Inchnadamh to Kylesku Ferry is resplendent with wild scenes of mountain and lochan, and eventually of Loch Glencoul. This picture shows the eastern flanks of Quinag which terminate with the lofty sentinel of Sail Gharbh. Its ascent by way of the Barrel Buttress is a problem even for the expert rock climber.

Glasven

(overleaf)

This massive mountain consists largely of quartzite and has little to offer either climber or walker. It appears on the right of the road to Kylesku.

Ben Stack from Loch More

Lairg is connected with Laxford Bridge by a
road that runs for miles along the shore of Loch
Shin. On leaving behind its rippling waters, the
scene changes dramatically, and the road enters a
conglomerate of Sutherland hills. Later it passes
three beautiful lochs and at the head of the last,
Loch More, it discloses the fine pyramid of Ben
Stack, as seen in this picture.

Arkle from Loch Stack

(overleaf)

This loch is said to be rich in salmon, and it lies between Ben Stack and Arkle. The latter mountain, consisting of quartzite, is known to mountaineers as a 'Slag Heap' – not worthy of exploration.

Foinaven from a roadside lochan

The drive from Laxford Bridge to Durness opens up long stretches of mountainous country, and from this roadside lochan it reveals the lofty ridge of Foinaven topping the skyline. While Foinaven also consists of quartzite, its ridge is rewarding for the climber, and undulates for nearly three miles to the east. A strong walker, accompanied by a climber who knows this terrain, should have no special difficulty in attaining the first of the several tops, from which can be seen the ridge trailing away in the direction of Ben Hope.

Sandwood Bay

(overleaf)

This bay, some distance to the south of Cape Wrath, is regarded by many as the most picturesque in Scotland. It can be reached from Kinlochbervie by car, followed by an easy walk.

Smoo Cave

This cave lies below the road going east from
Durness. There is a car-park on the left, from
which a path descends to the large opening
which can be entered safely at any time of day.

Ben Loyal from Lochan Hacoin

(overleaf)

This superb mountain rises from the swelling moorland some five miles to the south of Tongue, and its western front, when seen from the vicinity of Lochan Hacoin, makes one of the most striking pictures in Britain. Known also as the 'Queen of Scottish peaks', it is admired alike by artists and photographers. Its particular splendour is due to the graceful pendant ridges that join its four western peaks of granite; they impart to the whole of it a grandeur that is altogether out of proportion to its height.

147

The approach to Glen Affric

The beauty of this glen is world famous, and its loveliest section can be seen from a car. In late autumn, when the elegant birches are in their full glory, the masses of them at the entrance to the glen form a golden tapestry of unbelievable brilliance.

The highest point in the Glen
(overleaf)

The road climbs uphill through Glen Affric and when Loch Benevian is glimpsed ahead, its splendour amid the encircling trees is a delight to the eye. On reaching its highest point, the Kintail hills burst upon the view as a superb backdrop to this wonderful scene.

A burn of peaty water falls into the Loch
(overleaf p.154)

Water in its diverse forms has always interested me; here is an example of how a tiny piece of beautiful landscape can enchant the passer-by.

A quiet day by Loch Morlich

On the lofty plateaux of the Cairngorms are
many small lochs which to the passing walker
are like the flashing eyes of mountain gods. But
there are also many lochs of great charm on their
flanks, and one such is Loch Morlich, which lies
beside the road from Aviemore to Glenmore.
Ample parking allows the motorist to sit quietly
and admire its beauty.

The Cairn Gorm Range from Loch Morlich

This viewpoint is near the outflow of the loch, and is one of the few which has a clear foreground, disclosing a good view of the range. Cairn Gorm is on the extreme left, and the finest corrie, Coire an Lochain, is on the extreme right of the picture.

The view towards Braeriach from the summit of Cairn Gorm

(overleaf)

Since the chair-lift from the car-park in Coire Cas will lift the traveller to within 500 feet of the dominating peak, anyone who is fit should be able to walk up to the summit cairn and enjoy its extensive panorama. This picture shows how forlorn and bleak is the lofty plateau which extends as far as Ben Macdhui (its highest summit) and is backed from left to right by Cairn Toul, the Angel's Peak, and Braeriach. To the right of this is Cairn Lochan, the usual limit of a splendid day's walk along the ridge which can be taken by anyone.

An Lochain Uaine, Ryvoan

A short walk from Glenmore Lodge, near which
a car may be parked, brings one to this
enchanting lochan. Sitting beside it on a calm
day is a rewarding pleasure for the explorer of
these massive hills.

The Castle of Loch an Eilean

(overleaf)

This small loch is only a short distance from Aviemore, and is one of the chief attractions of the district.

Sgurr nan Gillean from Sligachan

I think it is true to say that Skye is our most beautiful island, and with the exception of Sleat it consists of barren undulating moorland from which rise our most spectacular mountains, the Coolins. Sleat is its most southerly peninsula and is usually regarded as the Garden of Skye, with more natural forest than the rest of the landscape. The whole coastline is indented by many lovely blue sea-lochs, and in fact no place is more than four or five miles from the sea. Its metropolis is the small, busy town of Portree, from which good roads radiate to every corner of the island and whose most important connection with the mainland is the ferry from

pinnacles project from its narrow crest, whose traverse is too difficult for any save the experienced mountaineer.

This should not deter the walker or the motorist from visiting Skye, for they will delight in the picturesque landscape and in the engirdling sea-cliffs which are nearly 1,000 feet high. After crossing the ferry to Kyleakin, the traveller should follow the coast road for about twenty-five miles, first passing through Broadford and then, with the Red Hills on the left, finally swinging round to Sligachan which is dominated by the splendour of Sgurr nan Gillean, as seen in this photograph.

Here he will find a first-class hotel which in my early days was patronized only by mountaineers and fishermen, whereas today it is the favoured hostelry of touring motorists. From its very doors the visitor can walk along Glen Sligachan to Loch Coruisk, with splendid hills on either side and a spectacular terminus of unparalleled wild beauty; or he can cross the low pass to Glen Brittle with the towering peaks of the Black Coolins on his left all the way. Should he prefer a drive, there is the complete circuit of the northern peninsula of Trotternish – the finest in Skye. The road goes north from Portree, passing below the precipices of the Storr with its conspicuous Old Man of Storr, runs for miles along the edge of the sea-cliffs, passes near Quiraing with its weird pinnacles, and then Flodigarry, one-time home of Flora MacDonald. Thence it follows the coast to the western side of Trotternish, with glimpses of the ruined castle of Duntulm and Uig with its graceful bay, followed by Kilmuir with Flora MacDonald's monument. Beyond this, a splendid road leads him quickly back to Portree.

The pinnacle ridge of Sgurr nan Gillean

(overleaf)

Kyle of Lochalsh, with road and rail links with Inverness. This misty isle is the Mecca of all British mountaineers, for there are no other great mountains (save perhaps Liathach and An Teallach) to compete with its serrated main ridge twisting southwards from Sligachan to Glen Brittle on the Atlantic coast. Innumerable

This photograph was taken late on an autumn afternoon from Sgurr a'Bhastier on the other side of the stony corrie. It shows the ridge whose traverse presents a notorious problem to the rock climber.

Coire na Creiche

One of the most magnificent corries in the Coolins, this is seen at its best from the path to Glen Brittle. Its central peak, Sgurr an Fheadain, is split vertically by the famous Waterpipe Gully, and is crowned by Bidein Druim na Ramh, one of the tricky obstacles encountered in the traverse of the Main Ridge.

The memorial hut in Glen Brittle

(overleaf)

This building was erected in 1963/4 by a Trust formed by the British Mountaineering Council and the Mountaineering Council of Scotland. It provides accommodation for visiting climbers at £1 a night, and is much appreciated by them because of the scarcity of beds in Glen Brittle. Rising in the background is Coire na Banachdich, which can be reached easily from this hut or the more distant campsite by any fit person; but to attain the lofty *Bealach* at its centre requires an intimate knowledge of its topography.

Coire Lagan

Sgurr Alasdair is the highest peak in the Coolins, and its ascent is usually made by way of the famous Stone Shoot which falls into this corrie. A walker can attain the corrie by a path from Glen Brittle, but few attempt the tough ascent of the Stone Shoot. Coire Lagan is a wonderful place in which to linger after a day on the ridges, and is so fascinating that many climbers have had to descend to the glen in the dark.

Marsco from the Sligachan Burn

(overleaf)

This shapely peak rises in isolation from the wilderness of Glen Sligachan and is one of its best-known landmarks. It is further down the glen than it looks from the hotel, but it may be ascended by any walker if he is accompanied by a climber who knows this terrain.

Glamaig

This beautiful conical peak stands almost at the
doors of the Sligachan Hotel, and its ascent
involves no difficulties other than slippery scree.

A cottage in Skye

(overleaf)

Every driver on his way to or from Portree passes this cottage which stands alone beside the road. Have you spotted it, dear reader?

The Storr from Loch Fada

This splendid rocky peak dominates the Trotternish skyline and is well seen from afar. It is about six miles to the north of Portree and its Old Man stands aloof from the formidable cliffs of the massif. There are three car-parks within easy reach, and from the Forestry Commission car-park below any pedestrian can attain the bizarre rock scenery surrounding the Inner Sanctuary. Exploring the ghostly pinnacles decking the Sanctuary is like wandering through the ruins of an ancient castle, whose long-dead occupants lurk behind every rock to observe the movements of the visitor.

The Quiraing Needle

Seen from afar, Quiraing does not disclose its weird scenery, but it can be reached from the sensational mountain road that crosses the Trotternish ridge from Staffin to Uig. The walk to it over grassland is a delight, with the towering cliffs ahead – its pinnacles and buttresses become more clearly defined during the approach, until finally the famous Needle rises into the sky as its most conspicuous feature.

The Bizarre Pinnacles of Quiraing

Walking in and out of these soaring rock
columns during the ascent to its remarkable
Table, is like wandering through a wonderland
of magic.

Duntulm from the West

(overleaf)

This historic ruin occupies an impregnable position overlooking the sea, but from its southern side it can easily be reached and explored. It was the one-time home of Donald Gorm, who, according to legend, was wounded by the last arrow left behind in Eilean Donan Castle, where he ultimately bled to death.

The deserted pier at Pooltiel

A very pleasant drive from Sligáchan follows the Dunvegan road, but deserts it before reaching the village and its famous castle of the MacLeods. It crosses the low hills about Glendale and, ignoring the left branch to Ramasaig, leads downhill to this charming spot with the beetling cliffs of Dunvegan Head opposite.

Waterstein Head

By following this road to its terminus on the far
western sea-cliffs of Skye, this prominent but
little-known headland can be seen dominating
the coastline and rising 971 feet above the waves
of the Atlantic.

The lighthouse on Neist Point

(overleaf)

A path from the car-park, high above the sea, leads to this lighthouse poised on the very edge of the cliffs. But its remarkable situation is seen at its best from the track going uphill from the car-park, as is shown by this picture.

189

Blaven from Loch Slapin

The long hilly drive from Broadford to Elgol unveils some magnificent views, and is a must for all visitors to Skye. This first dramatic scene appears on the approach to Loch Slapin, where the grandeur of the mountain group beyond it is seen at its best. The lofty ridges of Blaven, Clach Glas, and Sgurr nan Each make one of the finest rock traverses on the island.

The Long Ridge of Blaven

(overleaf)

This superb mountain ridge appears at its finest from the highest point of the path to Camasunary, which is a most interesting approach to the Coolins and Loch Coruisk. This walk involves no difficulties other than the 'Bad Step' near its terminus.

Beinn na Cro Reflected in Loch Slapin

A charming scene is revealed in retrospect from
the cottage standing on the edge of the loch,
near its narrows.

The Coolins
from Elgol
(overleaf)

This superb spectacle of the Coolins is suddenly
disclosed at the end of the road to Elgol, looking
across the immense blue foreground of Loch
Scavaig. When seen in favourable conditions, as
in this picture, it is considered by connoisseurs
as one of the finest in the world.

The Kilt Rock

(overleaf)

This can be seen by anyone driving north to Staffin Bay. The best viewpoint is a short step from the road, but care is essential when taking photos of it from the very edge of the cliffs, with the sea hundreds of feet below.

A Scottish sunset

Dramatic and colourful sunsets always have a special appeal, and those seen from the western Highlands are often of the finest. This was taken at Lairg. I was having dinner at the Sutherland Arms when it developed suddenly, and I hurried outside to photograph it at its transient best. A party of French tourists rushed out with their cameras just as it was fading – too late, to the great disappointment of them all!